Beyond Closure: Where Endings Sprout Wings

AF665016

Himanshi Jaglan

BookLeaf Publishing
India | USA | UK

Beyond Closure: Where Endings Sprout Wings © 2024 Himanshi Jaglan

All rights reserved.

No part of this publication may be reproduced, stored in a retrieval system, or transmitted, in any form or by any means, electronic, mechanical, photocopying, recording or otherwise, without the prior written permission of the presenters.

Himanshi Jaglan asserts the moral right to be identified as the author of this work.

Presentation by *BookLeaf Publishing*

Web: www.bookleafpub.com

E-mail: info@bookleafpub.com

ISBN: 9789360949150

First edition 2024

To you, the believer in magic and the seeker of wonder. This book is for your soul, to remind you of the extraordinary beauty that awaits amidst life's journey.

With love and enchantment,

Himanshi Jaglan

ACKNOWLEDGEMENT

I extend my heartfelt gratitude to my loved ones for their unwavering support, my readers for their encouragement, and the magic muse for my endless inspiration. Special thanks to those who caused endings in my life, for through their departure, I learned the art of letting go and embracing new beginnings without fear. Each ending paved the way for a better experience, allowing me to release fear, hatred, and rage, and to embark on fresh chapters of my life with renewed courage and hope.

Warm regards,
Himanshi Jaglan

PREFACE

Dear Reader,

Welcome to *Beyond Closure: Where Endings Sprout Wings*. As you embark on this enchanting journey through the realms of poetry, I invite you to leave behind the weight of the past and embrace the magic of new beginnings.

This collection of poems is more than just words on paper; it is a testament to the resilience of the human spirit and the boundless possibilities that await us when we dare to dream. Each verse is a tiny spark of fairy dust, lighting up the darkness and guiding us towards the light.

As you turn the pages, may you find solace in the beauty of the written word and inspiration in the power of imagination. May you discover within these lines a renewed sense of hope and a deeper understanding of the journey that lies ahead.

Thank you for joining me on this adventure. Together, let us explore the wonders of "Beyond Closure" and embrace the magic of new beginnings.

With love and fairy dust,

Himanshi Jaglan

DEDICATION

My Heart's Grateful Offering: A Journey Shared

In the tapestry of life, amidst its grand design,
I find solace in those whose love intertwines.
To my family, my cherished kin,
Whose love and support, from within.

Mom, siblings, each one dear,
In their embrace, I have no fear.
Tauji, Taiji, Chacha, Chachi, too,
Their presence, a blessing, through and through.

And to my dad, though he's not here,
His spirit lives on, ever near.
For I am his soul's reflection bright,

His blessings guide me, day and night.

To my friends, my beloved companions true,
Who've stood by me, in all I pursue.
Their laughter, their tears, their unwavering care,
Together we've weathered, life's every snare.

A special mention to Shammy sir and Ayushi ma'am,
Whose guidance and support, like a calming balm.
For making my vision, my first book, come alive,
With their wisdom and grace, my dreams thrive.

With hearts full of gratitude, I stand today,

In the company of those who light my way.
To each one mentioned, and those unnamed,
Your love and support forever proclaimed.

This is a gift from you to me, this book is a byproduct of your love and support.

And for you dear reader, this book is a gift to you from me.

In the pages of this book, I offer you a gift—a glimpse into my world, my heart, and the shared experiences that bind us together. With each word, I extend to you a piece of myself, a token of appreciation for your presence on this journey. As you unwrap the layers of these pages, may you discover the warmth of friendship, the comfort of understanding, and the joy of connecting with your own self and life. This book is my humble offering to you, dear reader, a gift from my soul to yours.

PART I

Awakening and Acceptance

Magic

Magic happens, believe, it's true,
In hearts where love's deep essence grew.
But how to measure love's embrace?
In magic's grace, we find its trace.

In smallest things, the light it gleams,
A river's flow, a poet's dreams,
The gentle touch, a baby's smile,
In life's sweet moments, all the while.

With open hearts, magic's near,
Tragic beauty, crystal clear,
Believe, it's there, in every way,
In every dawn, in night's array.

In your belief, the spark does start,
In every soul, in every heart,
So let it in, let it be known,
Magic's yours, in love it's sown.

Mind’s Makeover

In the realm of thoughts, a metamorphosis
awaits,
Where echoes of struggles and awakenings
resonate.
Lost, yet found, a cycle of rise and fall,
From shattered dreams to rising above it all.

My mind, a canvas, yearns for a transformation,
Crafting resilience amid life's tempestuous
narration.
Beneath the weight of trials, I've stumbled and
tripped,
But hope still flickers, through shadows, it's
slipped.

Dreams once bloomed, now lie in dormant slumber,
Stagnation pervades, casting a melancholic number.
Yet deep within, a flame, though faint, still glows,
Urging me to embrace the dreams that life bestows.

Scars etched on my heart, a reminder to be wary,
Fear encroaches, steering me towards sanctuary.
But I must trust the strength I've held before,
For in self-care and dreams, I'll find an open door.

Even amidst impossibility, I shall dare to dream,
Unafraid of failure, with a soul that gleams.
Through a life lived boldly, with no regrets in sight,
I'll fashion a tapestry woven with experiences bright.

So let the past guide, as I venture anew,
A mind's makeover, igniting skies of cobalt blue.
Embracing inner battles, with resilience unbound,
I'll awaken, transform, and in dreams, I'll be found.

Happiness, a gift of present

In shadows long, I sought your fleeting light,
Happiness, elusive, just out of sight.
Misconceptions veiled your simple grace,
But within my heart, you found your rightful place.

Not a person, thing, or tale to be told,
Yet a journey embarked, a friend to behold.
In perception's silence, you patiently reside,
A treasure within, in me, you'd always bide.

A component of existence, within my core,
You're not in the past or what the future has in store.
A gift of the present, a pure delight,
I see you now, in my heart's softest light.

I'll nurture you like my own soul's embrace,
For now, I know how to make you stay in place.
A part of myself, so still and serene,
Within me, you've always been, yet seldom
seen.

Happiness, you're the magic in clear eyes,
Cherished with love, as my spirit allies.
I found you when I made my spirit whole,
In every action, choice, you touched my soul.

Gratitude blossomed for each breath I drew,
A chance to change, to love, and to renew.
Insignificant in this vast cosmic space,
Yet my existence in this world finds its place.

Optimism, both a blessing and a bane,
Broke me down, but built me up again.
Through trials and tears, I found my own art,
Happiness, a journey within, a work of heart.

A human's existence, profound and found,
To feel life's richness, its beauty unbound.
Though the universe's mysteries vast and wide,
Within ourselves, happiness does reside.

So I journey onward, with this truth in tow,
In the warmth of my heart's ever-glow.

Discovering that happiness isn't far apart,
But within us, a treasure, a sacred work of art.

A journey to self-acceptance

Innocence adorned my youth's attire,
Carefree, I danced, my heart on fire.
A child so pure, in rose-colored dreams,
Life's gentle flow, in tenderest streams.

Yet, time's embrace, its wisdom cruel,
Imposed a change, a different rule.
Standards, society's weighty disguise,
Shackles and doubts, in others' eyes.

For I was deemed not quite enough,
To fit their mold, to play the bluff.
Innocence lost, their judgment I bore,
As my true self vanished more and more.

In their eyes, I needed to comply,
More of this, less of that, they'd imply.
To be embraced, loved, and understood,
I abandoned my essence, as best I could.

My laughter was silenced, my spirit confined,
In this painted world, my self declined.
To be adored, I wore a mask,
A puppeteer's show, a painful task.

A tale of courage and self-discovery

Hiding my light, in solitude I wept,
A lonely vigil, while the world slept.
The cage of insecurities, an iron vice,
Squeezing the joy from my very life.

Yet, deep inside, a spark remained,
A flicker of hope, once lost, now regained.
Courage ignited, I yearned to be whole,
To reclaim the child, regain my soul.

I turned my back on their hollow gaze,
Seeking the sun in solitary days.
The journey was arduous, filled with strife,
But I sought to embrace my truest life.

The world had expectations, its standards cruel,
But I'd forged a path, my essence my fuel.
Artists and kindred souls shared their insight,
Guiding me through the darkest night.

In hibernation and self-reflection's grace,
I found my truth in that secluded space.
Insecurities crumbled, like walls they fell,
I emerged as the one who'd broken the spell.

Today, I stand, a liberated me,
From the cage of insecurities, I'm free.
With strength and wisdom, my spirit takes flight,
A beacon of self-acceptance, shining bright.

Embracing the world with open eyes

Emerging from the cage of doubts and fears,
I stepped into a world with different gears.
A new perspective, a vision refined,
In this painted world, where lies entwined.

Life's canvas painted, a myriad of shades,
Fake smiles and facades in the grand parades.
A challenge anew, to stay true to my core,
Amidst the pretense, to seek something more.

With wisdom and courage, I navigate,
Through a world adorned in a glittering state.
Reminded always of what I hold dear,
The knowledge that kept me crystal clear.

In a realm of shadows, I stand with light,
Conscious and cautious in my earthly flight.

To remain authentic, to burn not in lies,
To lead by example, to be the wise.

In patience and peace, I'll continue to tread,
Knowing that souls, in shadows, may dread.
As I once did, lost in a world's masquerade,
Now, I'm a guide, from insecurities, unswayed.

With every step, my light I'll share,
A beacon of truth, in this world's affair.
Though paths may diverge, in time they'll align,
For self-acceptance, like stars, will shine.

As I journey onward, in this worldly space,
With an open heart, I'll embrace the race.
Guided by love, understanding, and grace,
I'll help others find their rightful place.

You are not alone

In the depths of my own journey, I tread,
A path of growth where my soul's widespread.
With each step forward, I thought I'd see,
The destination clear, the way to be free.

But here I stand, midst shadows and doubt,
Frustration's whispers, a challenging bout.
For every insight gained, another unfolds,
This quest for self, an infinite road, untold.

I chose this path, embraced the unknown,
To find the depths of self, where I've grown.
Yet today, impatience takes its toll,
A longing for rewards to fill my soul.

Oh, the lessons learned, the truths unveiled,
But still, a sense of being so derailed.
The vastness of this universe, it seems,
Mocks my efforts, haunts my dreams.

Yet I won't waver, won't step aside,
I'll walk this path, with arms open wide.
For even in frustration's relentless sway,
I know this journey's the only way.

To discover who I truly am within,
To shed the layers, to find what's been hidden.
So, to fellow seekers on this winding road,
Know you're not alone in this endless abode.

Though it's tiring and tests your might,
This path you've chosen, it leads to the light.
With every setback, every shift in your view,
You're growing stronger, and that's the truth
you'll accrue.

Embrace the journey, let patience be your guide,
In this vast sea of knowledge, let your spirit
glide.
For though it's challenging, you'll find your way,
Towards a brighter, wiser, and more resilient
day.

Lost, I wander

In the depths of my soul, emotions ignite,
Uncertain if this feeling is wrong or right.
For I'm merely human, with a heart that beats,
Embracing the emotions that make me complete.

Lost, I wander, unsure of my path's call,
Accomplishments archived, few to recall.
Yet, as a being, growth blossoms inside,
Questioning these feelings, seeking answers wide.

Overthinking swirls, anxiety takes hold,
But belief in unseen dreams consoles, I'm told.
Bursting from my bubble, I step into the day,
Encountering comfort, anxiety, and dismay.

Comparing myself to those who achieve,
Wealth and success, I struggle to believe.
But deep in introspection, I find solace there,
For my journey's purpose is beyond compare.

Though I may possess no earthly domain,
Nor a person to claim as my own, I remain.
These anxieties churn, yet within I find,
A world of peace, warmth, satisfaction combined.

Though accomplishments may seem out of reach,
I question my value, lessons that life teach.
Slowly I realize, on the right path I stride,
No need to rush, for magic will reside.

I stand firm in my desires, both real and grand,
Moving steadily, not stagnant, in life's grandstand.
Alive and resilient, I'll never lose my way,
Thoughts and strength empower, day after day.

In this poetic dance, I forge my own fate,
Defying demons, patience I cultivate.
With unwavering resolve, I strive to endure,
Slow but strong, my essence remains pure.

The journey continues, lessons I shall learn,
Growing, evolving, my soul's fire will burn.
For I am alive, embracing each thought,
Moving forward, with determination sought.

I am but a thread

In moments of provocation, when pushed to the edge,
My demons are unleashed, a battle to pledge.
Anger surges within, a fire burning bright,
Yearning to change the world with all my might.

I play dirty, I play politics, no rules to bind,
Fighting for my freedom, a stance that's defined.
I don't seek to prove a point with aggression,
If need be, I'll voice it with polite expression.

But when forced to conform to another's decree,
I'll fight and strive, using all that's within me.
My demons emerge, fierce and untamed,

A reminder that I know them, and how they're framed.

Yet amidst this rebellion, a feeling takes hold,
Amidst the chaos, a question, so bold.
Who am I to judge, to define what's right?
To impose my beliefs on others, extinguishing their light.

For within me lies insolence, a humble doubt,
Who am I to dictate, to cast others out?
To harm and hinder, for the sake of my own view,
When they, too, believe in what they hold true.

I stand firm in my beliefs, unwavering and strong,
But I respect their right to believe, to belong.
For in this vast world, opinions intertwine,
And I, just one soul, cannot solely define.

So I navigate this balance, with introspection deep,
Embracing my demons, and the doubts that creep.
Knowing that in the tapestry of life's complex scene,
I am but a thread, a part of the grander scheme.

In the moment

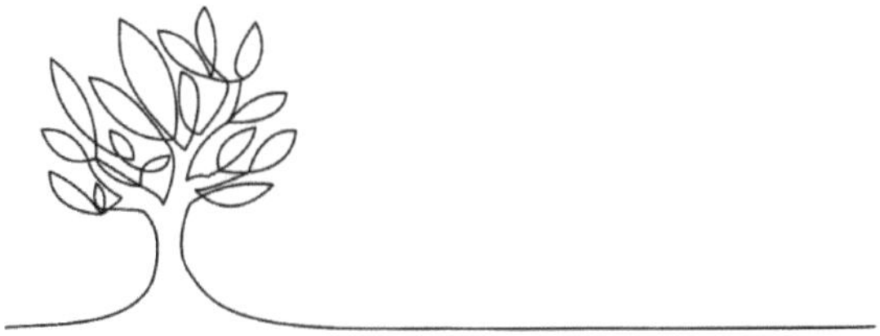

Ice cream melts,
Sky ablaze,
Fields kissed by rain,
Nature's grace.

Water's mirror,
Fields after rain,
Van Gogh's art,
Reflecting beauty, a masterpiece start.

In my car,
Melodies play,
BTS's Spring Day,
Guiding my way.

Homeward bound,
Heart aglow,
Finding peace,
Where dreams grow.

Coming home,
A place serene,
Soul's delight,
A tranquil scene.

Sun's orange ball,
In sky's embrace,
A radiant glow,
Upon my face.

Sundae's delight,
Black Forest's embrace,
Sweet and sour melody,
Berries and brownie's grace.

The pearl

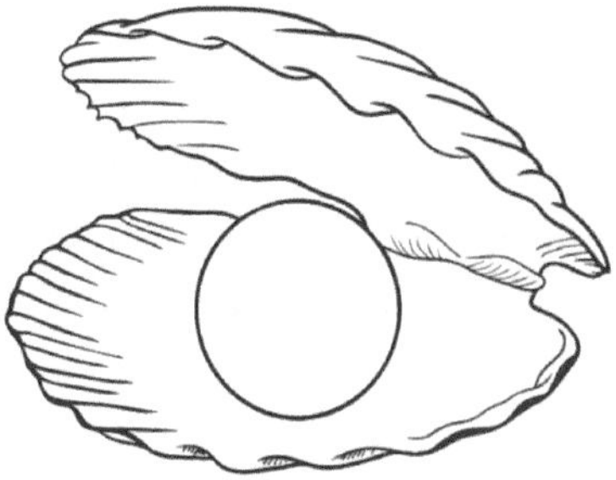

In a world where boundaries tried to confine,
I emerged, like a pearl, from the depths divine.
Once hidden away, kept from daring dreams,
But my heart ignited, with fierce, fiery streams.

Every scar I carry, a tale to be shared,
Each mark on my skin, a story, unimpaired.
Longing for adventures, eager to explore,
Yearning for the unknown, craving so much
more.

Told to be delicate, fragile and small,
But my spirit was fierce, refusing to fall.
I embarked on a journey, fearless and bold,
Unveiling mysteries, my own truth to behold.

Through 28 years of trials and quests,
I discovered strength in a woman's behest.

Not the men who were bold, but women who thrived,
In their femininity, their power revived.

Once longing to be like boys, to be men,
Now grateful for being born a woman, again.
Embracing the balance of feminine grace,
I adore the strength found within this space.

No longer complaining, no more despair,
For I revel in the beauty that we all share.
With delicate makeup, and heels that I wear,
I embody strength, a force beyond compare.

Two worlds entwined, in harmony they sway,
A creature of beauty, who can fiercely portray.
I love myself now, for the woman I've become,
Thankful for each step, every battle I've won.

Gratitude to the universe, to God above,
For crafting me with a fierce feminine love.
And to the women who guided my way,
For teaching me courage, every single day.

To the men who cherished and embraced my soul,
For their love and support that made me whole.
I stand here today, a woman so free,
Radiant and beautiful, embracing all of me.

In high heels or bare feet, I'll captivate your
gaze,
Surprising the world with my remarkable ways.
I celebrate being a woman, strong and divine,
A pearl that emerged from life's vast design.

PART II
Healing and Forgiveness

Forgiving myself

In the depths of emotions, a story unfolds,
Mistakes made, chances untold.
With a heavy heart, I confess my wrong,
A tale of love's hold, freedom withdrawn.

In the name of love, I took her hand,
To shield her from pain, I couldn't withstand.
Her ache would break me, I was afraid to see,
But in my protection, I failed to let her be.

Forgetting her pain was a chance to grow,
To learn, to forge a path, her own story to sow.
In my quest to shield, I stifled her song,
Robbed her of experiences, where she belonged.

Realizing now, the depth of my mistake,
Her pain was her journey, her path to take.
A chance to blossom, to rise above,
But in my fear, I robbed her of self-love.

In the name of love, I tried to protect,
But in doing so, her growth I neglect.

Her story untold, her spirit confined,
In the shelter of my love, her freedom confined.

Let this be a lesson, a poignant refrain,
That pain is a teacher, not meant for disdain.
For in the depths of struggle, we find our own
voice,
To rise, to conquer, to make our own choice.

May love's embrace be gentle and kind,
Allowing each soul to flourish, to find.
The strength to endure, the wisdom to see,
That pain is a chance to grow, to truly be free.

In the name of love, let us understand,
To honor each journey, to lend a helping hand.
For in embracing pain, we foster growth,
And in letting go, we find love's oath.

So, in love's binding chains,
Let hearts find solace, release from pains.
May this song be a reminder true,
To honor love's freedom, in all we do.

Why should I fear?

What do I fear in this endless race?
Will my tales dry up, vanish in empty space?
Why hold worries close, so tight and near?
Will stories flow, free from doubt and fear?

I questioned myself, gripped by uncertainty,
But within, I found answers with clarity.

A past as vast as the boundless sea,
Present alive, filled with joyful glee.
Unknown adventures, soaring high,
Imagination thriving, reaching the sky.

Boredom has no hold, my spirit soars free,
Magic and love, in every moment I see.

Why then fear in this realm of grace?
My stories will endure, leaving their trace.

Within me, inspiration blooms and grows,
Creativity finds solace, wherever it flows.
Let go of fear, unlock the wonders I possess,
A spirit unbound, a life filled with finesse.

So I'll share my tales, with passion and zeal,
The depth of my emotions, genuinely revealed.
No fear of running dry, for within me it resides,
A universe of stories, where creativity abides.

Healing amidst frustration

Each fear faced, a lesson learned anew,
Strength tested, as challenges grew.
Motivational words, they echo near,
But scars from the past, they still adhere.

Every day, seeking light and hope,
Yet fear persists, its grip won't elope.
Brave steps taken, hearts filled with might,
Yet stumbling again, in the darkness of night.

Pain deepens with each fall and bruise,
Healing slower, a battle I choose.
Though I know I'm wiser, stronger inside,
This time, patience is my faithful guide.

It takes longer, I admit with a sigh,
To muster courage, fears to defy.
Yet I understand, it's part of the way,
Embracing frustration, as I find my own sway.

Impatience may linger, testing my will,
But I'll be patient, as time stands still.
For wounds this deep, they need their space,
To heal completely, at their own pace.

In the face of adversity

In the depths of despair, hope flickers bright,
With every stumble, just live, embrace the fight.
What once seemed lost, can be found again,
Believe, my friend, in the power to regain.

Failures may come, like waves crashing ashore,
But with every stumble, just live, strive for more.
For within the heart, resilience takes root,
A seed of perseverance, bearing hopeful fruit.

Though hardships persist, with unwavering might,
With every stumble, just live, ignite your light.
For in the face of adversity, strength prevails,
Each setback, a stepping stone as the story unveils.

Yes, you may falter, stumble along the way,
But with every stumble, just live, don't dismay.
Stay consistent, keep moving with resolve,
And watch as life's tapestry begins to evolve.

The journey is rife with pain and sorrow's sting,
But with every stumble, just live, let emotions sing.
Feel the richness of life's vibrant hue,
With each passing moment, growth will accrue.

So, my dear friend, with courage to strive,
With every stumble, just live, keep hope alive.
For in the tapestry of life's intricate design,
Thrives a spirit unyielding, resilient, and divine.

A day will come, when joy will bloom anew,
With every stumble, just live, dreams come true.
Through the depths of emotions, both highs and lows,
Embrace them fully, for it's in living that life grows.

So, live, my friend, with every beat of your heart,
With every stumble, just live, embrace your part.
For within the journey, hope forever thrives,
And in the act of living, your spirit truly thrives.

Song of longing heart

In solitude, she walks a path unknown,
Strong, yet burdened, her struggles not shown.
Not pretending strength, but concealing the ache,
Longing for love, a tender touch to partake.

She stands tall, facing the battles alone,
Yearning for warmth, a love to call her own.
Not seeking grand gestures or riches untold,
Just someone by her side, their hand to hold.

A gentle hug, a soothing balm for her soul,
A respite from the world, making her feel whole.
The ache in her heart, the longing deep within,
For tender moments shared, where true love begins.

She's not afraid of standing on her own,
But craves understanding, a love softly shown.
To be seen and cherished for who she truly is,
With tenderness and care, to find eternal bliss.

In the depths of her being, she yearns for respite,
A hand to hold, to feel love's gentle light.
No need for grand words or a lavish display,
Just someone who sees her, in their own special
way.

She's strong, yes, but her heart longs for release,
To feel understood, to find inner peace.
To be traced in love's comforting embrace,
To find solace and refuge in a tender space.

For in her depth, beneath her warrior's guise,
She's a woman longing for love's gentle ties.
To lay down her burdens, if only for a while,
And bask in the warmth of a loving smile.

So she carries on, facing each new day,
With hope in her heart, yearning in every way.
For that tender love, so pure and divine,
A connection that tells her, she's not alone in
this rhyme.

Burdens of heart

In the depths of heart burdens we bear,
We carry the weight, the pain, the despair.
We hesitate to burden others with our plight,
Knowing they have their own battles to fight.

But hear me, dear friend, I understand,
The heaviness that grips you, the pain firsthand.
For I too have walked this treacherous path,
Felt the weight of failures and sorrows amassed.

You don't have to speak, I can sense it all,
Even when you hide, I can hear your heart's call.
So fear not the act of hiding away,
It's a shield, a sanctuary where emotions sway.

You can hide all you want, I'll patiently wait,
Until you're ready to unlock fate.

I know it's not an act, but a longing to find,
A place of solace, where your soul can unwind.

Even if you don't tell, I can feel it in my core,
Even if you hide, I can sense it, I implore.
So don't be afraid, my friend, to retreat,
Take all the time you need, in your haven, find a seat.

But remember, as you hide, I'll wait outside,
For I trust you'll come out, and in me confide.
Together we'll face the world, hand in hand,
And forge a victory of your own, on solid land.

Home awaits, my friend, beyond the veil,
A sanctuary where your heart will prevail.
Find the courage within, let it guide your way,
Step out from your hiding, embrace the light of day.

I know it, I can feel it, your strength deep within,
So come, my dear friend, let the healing begin.
Together we'll journey, to a place called home,
Where love, acceptance, and solace will forever roam.

Embracing the journey

In the depths of darkness, where shadows reside,
I offer you my courage, my strength, by your side.
For I understand the pain that dwells within,
And I'm here to ignite the flame, let the healing begin.

With every step you take, I'll be right there,
Gathering courage from the world, so rare.
I see you, my friend, I sense your despair,
Together, we'll conquer, this burden we'll bear.

I offer you hope, like a guiding light,
To dispel the darkness, to make things right.
For within you lies a strength untold,
A spirit so resilient, a heart so bold.

Don't give up, my friend, on this journey of the soul,
You possess the power to make yourself whole.
I'm waiting outside, observing with care,
Gathering all the courage, the world can share.

I can feel your struggles, your battles untold,
The weight of your demons, the stories unfold.
But know that you're not alone, I stand by your side,
Together, we'll face the darkness, with courage as our guide.

Take my hand, my friend, let's walk this path,
Embrace the journey, let go of the wrath.
I offer you my strength, my unwavering belief,
That within you lies the power to find relief.

With every breath you take, let the healing flow,
Unleash your spirit, let your true self glow.
I'll be your constant companion, your unwavering cheer,
As you embrace the journey, conquering every fear.

Know that I'm here, with hope in my heart,
Witnessing your transformation, a work of art.
So gather your strength, my friend, let's begin,

The journey of healing, where new beginnings win.

Triumph of heart

Behold, dear friend, a transformation in sight,
From caterpillar's struggle to butterfly's flight.
I see it in you, the readiness to soar,
To step out of darkness, to open new doors.

Take my hand, let's walk this journey together,
As we conquer the dark, no matter the weather.
The path may be thorny, the road may be long,
But with each step we take, we grow ever
strong.

I know you're wounded, tired, and worn,
But fear not, my dear, for a new day is born.
This transformation, it took all your might,
But the world outside offers energy and light.

With new eyes, let's see the world unfold,
Where prosperity flies and dreams take hold.
Though challenges remain, we'll face them head-on,
For you are not alone, you've never been alone.

I walk ahead, clearing the path for you,
Guiding you forward, our dreams in view.
Though thorns may prick, skies above are clear,
Each step brings magic, dispelling every fear.

In every breath, find peace, love, and warmth,
As the journey unfolds, embracing its worth.
Allow my embrace to replenish your soul,
As you embark on this journey, making it whole.

Our paths may diverge, yet deep in your heart,
Know that you're never alone, even when worlds apart.
For every path you choose, there are others in tow,
Leading, supporting, or walking with you, they'll show.

Trust in yourself, my friend, for you hold the key,
To triumph over darkness, to set your spirit free.
I believe in you, in the strength you possess,

I see you, I understand you, your struggles I
address.

Together, we'll conquer, hearts united as one,
Unleashing the power that within you is spun.
So hold my hand, let's pave this path anew,
Triumph of the heart, together, we'll see it
through.

Song of my silly heart

In the rhythm of my life, I dance,
With a jazzy beat, I take a chance.
My silly heart, it flutters and sings,
With every tune, joy it brings.

Oh, sweet joy surrounds me like a song,
By simple things, I can't go wrong.
A laugh, a stroll, a sunlit day,
They bring delight in their own playful way.

Butterflies dance, they join my flight,
In clouds of bliss, we take delight.
Embracing grace, their tender embrace,
I soar with joy, in a magical chase.

Now, the urge to sing, this song inside,
I leap with joy, in my heart I confide.
Blessings showered upon me from above,
I jump with joy, embraced by self-love.

The greatness of being born, it fills my mind,
I lead myself to joy, it's my own kind.
People I've met on this journey so far,
Their presence adds sparkle, like a guiding star.

Giggles and jumps, surrounded by glee,
Moments with loved ones, forever with me.
Love cherished, forever so dear,
And I jump with joy, knowing I steer.

Oh, my silly heart, not foolish at all,
You guide me to joy, standing tall.
In my heart, I find this power divine,
A melodic symphony, where joy intertwines.

In the rhythm of my life, I dance,
A sweet melody, taking every chance.
With my silly heart as my guiding light,
I embrace the magic, shining so bright.

Miracles of life

Amidst complaints, I failed to see,
The blessings surrounding me.
Now I embrace, with heart's decree,
Life's magic, a sight to set me free.

Grateful for each day anew,
Miracles of life in view.
Believing in magic's grace,
In different forms, life will embrace.

Veiled Core

Within the night's embrace, we endure,
Till morning's song fills this space so pure.
Yet within me lies a darkness, unseen,
concealed,
Where secrets dwell, forever unrevealed.

A fortress I've erected, guarding what's inside,
Hidden depths where shadows and secrets abide.
Only by breaching the walls, piercing through
the veil,
Can one explore the depths where darkness
prevails.

Is it a chasm of despair or a realm of sublime
grace?
Beyond those walls, no one can truly embrace.
For none have dared to venture into the
unknown,
Leaving unanswered questions, seeds of the soul
sown.

In this realm of mystery, secrets tightly sealed,
Yearning for one brave enough, whose spirit's revealed.
But alas, the truth remains concealed, unclaimed,
For no one yet has crossed the walls I've framed.

Embrace the Stumble

In the depths of despair, where hope seems to stray,
With each stumble, rise, and sway.
When life's burdens weigh heavy on your chest,
Know, my friend, you're not alone in this quest.

As darkness descends and dreams lose their glow,
Let hope's river flow.
Within your soul, a flame burns bright,
Embrace it, ignite it, guide your flight.

Though storms may rage, casting shadows long,
Keep your secrets strong.
Believe in the strength that lies deep within,
A warrior's spirit, ready to win.

When heartache grips and tears gently fall,
Stand firm and tall.
Tomorrow's dawn holds promises anew,
With fresh opportunities waiting for you.

In chaos's grip, seek solace deep,
Let life's tapestry sweep.
Discover the magic in stories untold,
As life's wonders gently unfold.

In the darkest of nights, hope still prevails,
Break free from life's trails.
Each day brings a chance to renew,
To rise above challenges, to pursue.

So, dear friend, when hope seems to wane,
Banish the pain.
In adversity's face, let strength arise,
Guiding us through, with hope as our prize.

With fervor, with courage, with might,
Hold on tight.
For within each struggle, beauty is found,
And through every stumble, new dreams
abound.

Embrace the Light Within

Hush, my soul, don't despair,
Listen closely, feel the air,
It's my heart, dear soul, I say,
Love awaits in every way.

With each beat, a love reborn,
Embracing life, no need to mourn,
In the depths, a love so pure,
Endless cycles, love will endure.

Trust in me, your beating core,
Love's strength, a boundless store,
With every whisper, we'll ignite,
Love's flame, burning bright.

So, my soul, don't be afraid,
In love's embrace, we'll cascade,
Hearts entwined, we'll find our role,
Together, we'll rise and console.

PART III
Letting Go and Moving On

Accepting myself

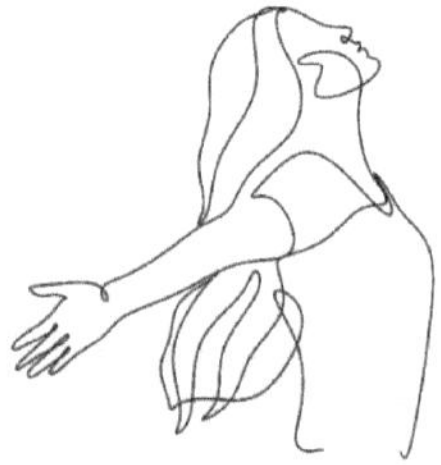

You! I lost you, the weaker side of me.
You, who was fooled, betrayed, I couldn't see.
You, of whom I'm ashamed, filled with regrets,
But now I accept you, and my strength resets.

You, a part I denied, it's time to embrace,
For through understanding, I find my grace.
You, the past version of who I used to be,
I'll accept and grow, and set myself free.

Desires

Saintly or Satanly?
My desire, a flame that burns sincerely.
In life's journey, it's my guide,
Quenching thirst, I won't hide.

DESIRE, a word with power,
Ignites the heart, a thrilling hour.
"Control your desires," they decree,
But taking charge, I am free.

Which one is it, you ask of me?
It's the desire to be fearlessly,
To take control, and not suppress,
Embracing passions, I must confess.

I'm giving in to my desires,
No longer haunted by false empires.
For in their pursuit, I find my way,
Living life fully, every single day.

After all, what is a life without desire?
A dull existence, quenched fire.
So I choose to dance with my own firelight,
In desires' embrace, my spirit takes flight.

Dreams' Eternal Symphony

In my world of dreams, where reality blends,
Where magic and wonder know no ends.
Imaginations soar, and desires take flight,
A symphony of dreams, a captivating sight.

Within these realms, my heart finds solace true,
A tapestry of visions, both old and new.
Parisian streets and fashion's vintage grace,
A world where beauty thrives in every place.

Cafes and bakeries, a culinary delight,
Where flavors dance, and senses take flight.
Restaurants adorned with elegance and charm,
A feast for the soul, a romantic balm.

In this realm, alchemy weaves its spell,
Harnessing the elements, a power to compel.
A hero's journey, to save the world's plight,
Bringing harmony and love's guiding light.

But amidst these dreams, a longing remains,
For love's embrace, where hearts intertwine.
Prince Charming, the one to hold my hand,
A connection so deep, forever to withstand.

Two worlds collide, reality and fantasy,
A kaleidoscope of dreams, a symphony.
From twinkling stars to sunlit skies,
Nature's art unfolds before my eyes.

Raindrops fall, a symphony on the ground,
A symphony of colors, a world so profound.
Lands of green and meadows in bloom,
A painted canvas, dispelling all gloom.

These dreams, my refuge, my eternal flame,
Igniting my heart, love's undying claim.
In this world where reality and fantasy reside,
Forever I'll dream, with love and warmth as my guide.

Whispers of the Soul

In the depths of my soul, a story untold,
A melody of life, in whispers it unfolds.
Beneath the surface, where shadows reside,
Lies a world unseen, where secrets hide.

In the stillness of night, when stars align,
I unveil my truth, layer by layer, line by line.
In quiet moments, when no one's around,
I let my heart speak, with a gentle sound.

Oh, the rhythm of my life, intricately composed,
Each note reflects the journey I've chosen.
With every step I take, in this dance divine,
I discover the essence of what makes me shine.

In highs and lows, triumphs and tears,
I find solace in conquering my fears.
Through laughter and pain, joy and ordeal,
I embrace the essence of my vibrant zeal.

In the depths of my soul, I've found my own way,
A symphony of moments, where dreams hold sway.
Within me lies a universe, vast and profound,
Where authenticity reigns, my truth unbound.

So let this be a reflection, testament to my soul,
A reservoir of resilience, of who I've become and whole.
With profound understanding, I share with the world,
The journey of self-discovery, where I am unfurled.

Danger's kiss

Does danger birth beauty, or beauty breeds peril?
A question that stirs, as my thoughts unfurl.
In the dance of risk, my spirit takes flight,
Embracing the unknown with all of its might.
With each daring step, my heart skips a beat,
In pursuit of dreams, both wild and sweet.
For within the allure of life's thrilling embrace,
I find the essence of beauty in every chase.
So let the world marvel at its perceived risk,
While I savor the moments, both daring and brisk.
For it is in the harmony of danger and delight,
That I discover the true magic of life's twilight.

Guardian of Light

Fear not the goodness given, a gift so rare and true,
For it holds the power to transform, to renew.
In the face of doubt, let your compassion shine,
Illuminate their world, with love's embrace divine.

For their fire lies dormant, awaiting your gentle touch,
To ignite their souls, and release them from the clutch
Of icy winters past, where hearts were cold and still,
Your warmth rekindles hope, against all odds, uphill.

Give without expectation, with open hands and heart,
But remember to protect your own flame, a precious part.

If you've given more than received, don't dwell in dismay,
Move forward, knowing you've brightened someone's way.

Hold this truth within your heart, safe and sound,
And continue your journey, with a lighter weight unbound.

Embrace this noble duty, with courage as your guide,
For through your acts of kindness, their spirits shall abide.

And as their flames awaken, a symphony will start,
A dance of souls united, forever in your heart.
So cherish this calling, though unsought, yet bestowed,
As you kindle their fire, with love's vibrant ode.

For together you'll shine, a testament of light,
In this wondrous journey, where goodness takes flight.
Give without expectation, a selfless gift so grand,
But remember to nourish your own fire, hand in hand.

Move forward with grace, leaving regrets behind,
With a heart that's full, and a spirit unconfined.
Know this and keep it close, in your heart's safe embrace,
As you journey onward, leaving a trail of love and grace.

And as you give and receive, in this beautiful art,
May your fire burn bright, illuminating every heart.

Chasing love's thrill

I still yearn for a love that brings a thrill,
Igniting fireworks, a heart's dance so surreal.
A love like no other, craving it more and more,
An insatiable desire that leaves me wanting more.
I long for a love like a fairy tale's bliss,
A prince with a magical touch, a dreamlike kiss.
A love that brings joy tinged with a hint of fear,
A love that races my heart when it draws near
A love that feels fresh, with each passing day,
Surprises aplenty, never fading away.
A love that excites, never ceasing to ignite,
An eternal flame that keeps my spirit alight.
Like the moon, forever bound to the earth,
A love so strong, defying distance and dearth.

A love as beautiful as cherry blossoms in bloom,
Both enchanting and haunting, casting a spell of doom.
A love like a breaking dawn, gentle and serene,
A morning song that whispers love's sweetest dream.
A love etched in stories, timeless and true,
Engraved in the depths of oceans, an eternal view.
A love woven in melodies, harmonies divine,
Cold monsoon winds that sweep me, love so fine.
A love seemingly distant, but closer than I perceive,
Bringing galaxies of emotions, causing my heart to heave.
Longing for this love makes my heart ache,
Why do I crave it, this love for heaven's sake?
Am I destined to fall for dangerous things?
A love promising eternity, no broken wings.
I seek a love yet unfound, a dream unreal,
Wondering if my heart's desires will ever reveal.
For if such a love exists, even in my wildest dreams,
I'll embrace it with open arms, or so it seems.
I like winters, summers, and monsoons too,
Darkness brings fear, yet an allure I pursue.
Thunders and storms bring a calming grace,

Strength coexists with weakness, a delicate embrace.
Jumping off cliffs, a thrilling risk I take,
The thrill in the air, the thrill that makes me wake.
I'll land safe or broken, and mend myself anew,
For I'm unafraid of love, a leap I'll pursue.
I'll take that fall, again and again,
Learning to soar high, in love's sweet domain.
With a wish that should come true, I'll persist,
Finding a love that fulfills, forever to exist.

Forging Forgiveness

In the depths of trust, a revelation so stark,
When a loved one's facade crumbled in the dark.
My heart, once trusting, now shattered and frail,
Betrayed by deceit, as illusions unveiled.

Doubt and anguish clouded my weary mind,
As I questioned the essence of humankind.
How could someone I cherished, so close to my
core,
Turn out to be someone I knew no more?

Reflecting on the signs I chose to ignore,
Blinded by affection, my judgment was poor.
Their actions spoke volumes, yet I chose to
deny,
The truth staring back, hidden in their lie.

But dwelling on betrayal only deepens the pain,
So I choose forgiveness, to break free from disdain.
Accepting their flaws, their struggles, their strife,
I release the burden and reclaim my life.

Forgiveness isn't easy, nor does it come quick,
But it's the path to healing, the ultimate pick.
For in forgiving others, we set ourselves free,
From the chains of resentment, we find serenity.

I give myself space to heal and to grow,
To let go of the past and embrace what's to show.
With forgiveness as my compass, I chart a new course,
Guided by grace, with resilience as my force.

Though scars may linger, they won't define me,
I'll rise above the pain, stronger than I used to be.
For in forgiveness lies power, a beacon of light,
Leading me forward, into the endless night.

So I forgive and I let go, with an open heart,
Choosing love over bitterness, a brand new start.
Embracing the journey, with courage as my creed,
Forging forgiveness, in every word and deed.

The Journey of Choice

In a world of choices, vast and undefined,
I embarked on a journey, seeking clarity to find.
Step by step, I ventured forth, unsure yet steadfast,
Trusting my instincts, on the path that would last.

Amidst uncertainty, I questioned every turn,
Examining each choice, eager to discern.
Listening closely to the whispers within,
Guided by intuition, where true wisdom begins.

At first, doubts lingered, hesitation prevailed,
But I silenced the noise, and courage unfurled.
For in the depths of my being, I found the key,

To unlock the power of choice, to set myself
free.

With each decision, I leaned into trust,
Embracing authenticity, shedding doubt's crust.
No longer seeking validation from outside,
I honored my truth, with newfound pride.

Through challenges and trials, I persevered,
Knowing that within me, strength always
appeared.
I learned to let go of fears that held me back,
And embraced the journey, despite any lack.

Now, with confidence blooming, I walk my own
way,
Making choices aligned with my truth every day.
I encourage you, dear reader, to heed this call,
Trust in yourself, and rise above all.

For in the journey of choice, lies a path to
unfold,
Where authenticity reigns, and stories are told.
So listen to your heart, let your intuition guide,
And embrace the journey, with joy by your side.

Realization

In the depths of contemplation, a truth emerged,
No longer confined by the past, my spirit surged.
I felt sorry and angry for what was done,
But dwelling in those emotions, my present was undone.
Gradually, forgiveness became my guiding light,
Yet, it was no easy task to relinquish the fight.
Rage, anger, and resentment ran deep within,
Weeding them out, a battle to begin.
But as I questioned my role, a realization was revealed,
I, too, played a part, wounds yet to be healed.
Weakness allowed others to overpower my might,
Seeking sympathy, I gave away my own inner light.

In someone else's story, guilt and blame we share,
Realizing my choices, my own burdens to bear.
Belief and intuition became my guiding star,
Though mistakes were made, growth took me far.

Forgetting

Letting go, a challenge of profound depth,
Releasing resentment, sorrow, and regrets that crept.
Miserable and weighed down, I longed for release,
Seeking peace and happiness, a path to find solace.
Acceptance whispered its gentle decree,
What's done is done, and can no longer be.
I embraced the lessons, leaving the pain behind,
Choosing growth and transformation, a new mindset to find.
In the realm of forgetting, I found clarity's embrace,
No longer seeking external sources to trace.

Accepting the good and the bad, I embarked on
a new quest,
To be better, wiser, and face life's behest.
With each step, clarity illuminated my way,
Internal wisdom guiding me, no need to stray.
The burdens of the past began to fade,
A brighter future, my heart eagerly made.

Letting Go

Letting go, a gradual release from the chains,
Acceptance leading the way, as resilience
remains.
Step by step, I moved forward with grace,
Contentment found, in my own chosen space.
Unbeknownst to me, letting go had begun,
Acceptance and progress, hand in hand, were
spun.
Moving forward, guided by acceptance's light,
Releasing the past, embracing a future so bright.
In the journey of letting go, I found my stride,
With each step, a sense of freedom amplified.
No longer held captive by what once held me
back,
I embraced the present, courageously on track.
The realization, forgiveness, forgetting, and
letting go,
A symphony of emotions, a transformative flow.

Through each stage, I found wisdom's gentle call,
Guiding me to a place where contentment does enthrall.
This is the journey I embarked upon, filled with strife,
Yet, with each step, I discovered a vibrant new life.
In the depths of realization, forgiveness, forgetting, and release,
I found the strength within, a sense of inner peace.

PART IV
Embracing Life's Essence

Melodic Ode to Life

Oh, how I cherish my life, a symphony divine,
A tapestry of moments, each one is mine.
From the gentle purr of my beloved cat's
embrace,
To children's laughter, filling every space.

Animals captivate me, stealing my heart,
Their innocence and charm, a work of art.
Feeding a cow a banana, a humorous delight,
Unpeeling it unknowingly, a funny sight.

Rain and thunderstorms, nature's magical
embrace,
The darkened sky, an enchanting grace.
The thunder's roar, the lightning's dance,
Nature's symphony, a mesmerizing trance.

In twilight's embrace, the day gently fades,
Lights twinkle, casting dreams on serenades.
Early morn, the sun's golden glow,
Birds serenade, as morning dew bestows.

November's scent, citrusy and bright,
Sweet and tangy, a fragrance of delight.
Winter's pleasure, savoring hot cocoa's bliss,
Sipping slowly, warming the soul's abyss.

Spring's awakening, nature's jubilee,
Blooms and blossoms, a vibrant decree.
Summer's warmth, ripe mango's kiss,
Light attire, a carefree summer's bliss.

Winter's chill, fashion takes a leap,
Classy ensembles, confidence runs deep.
The color black, an aura of power,
Elegance personified, a timeless tower.

Festivals abound, joy fills the air,
Teej's hennaed hands, Diwali's flair.
Exchanging gifts, spreading love's embrace,
Celebrating life, in every vibrant space.

Cafés and coffee, a soothing delight,
Matcha latte in hand, a sip of respite.
Under a tree, nature's beauty I view,

Fashion's parade, skies painted anew.

Books, windows to worlds beyond,
Whispering tales, enchantment spawned.
Poetry's rhythm, a balm for the soul,
Melodies of words, making me whole.

BTS, a melody that echoes deep,
Their smiles and voices, a dream's keep.
Inspiration flows, dreams take flight,
"BTS Forever," a beacon of light.

Love in all its forms, a magical dance,
Embracing hearts, love's sweet romance.
Children's laughter, a symphony untamed,
Pets and owners, a bond forever proclaimed.

Majestic mountains, nature's grandeur,
Journey's path, an adventure pure.
Long drives, music guiding the way,
Embracing the unknown, where hearts sway.

In every moment, in each joy and strife,
Love for life, the rhythm of my life.
A melodic ode to the beauty I find,
A celebration of life forever intertwined.

Embracing Love's Essence

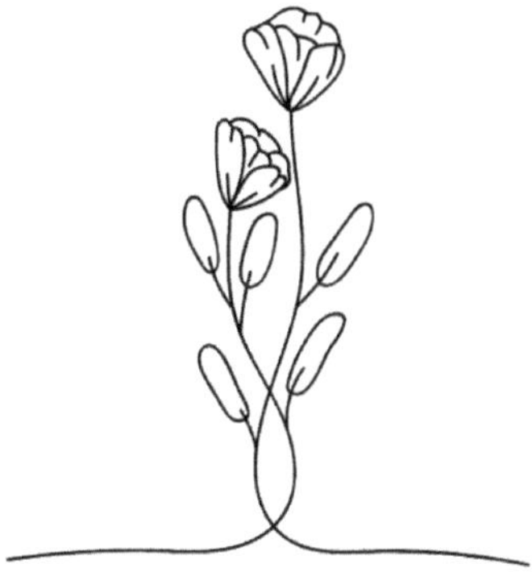

In the beginning, wanting and needing,
Love's journey, ever proceeding,
Giving, losing, the heart conceding,
Embracing, feeling, love's soul, I'm heeding.

I am love, I've come to find,
In myself, love's truth aligned,
Embodying it, soul entwined,
In love's arms, my heart defined.

I know, it may not make much sense,
But this love is my self-defense,
A dance of love, a sweet suspense,
In me, love's essence, immense.

Embracing Life's Dance

In life's sweet tale, we find our way,
Laughing, crying, day by day.
Embrace the journey, heart aglow,
Love's tender dance, it'll bestow.

With every turn, new faces near,
Cherish each moment, hold them dear.
Life's ebb and flow, a wondrous art,
Live with love, and an open heart.

Disguise

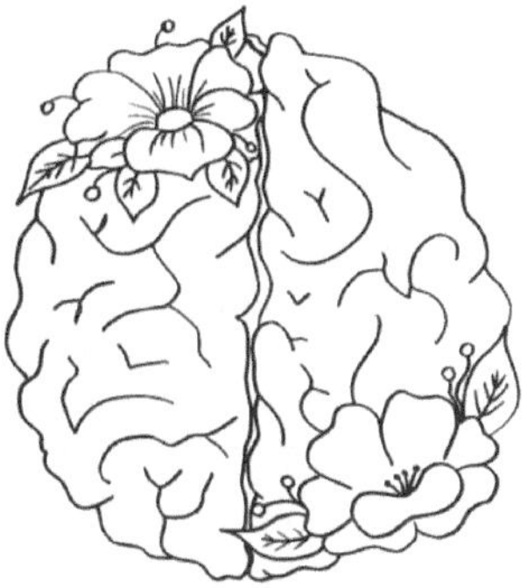

Sky,
Dark clouds,
Rainbows,
Roses and thorns
Dandelions
Butterflies and bugs
Lightning
Unrequited yet justified.

So many words said, much feelings expressed.

Stillness.

DISGUISE.

stone cold or alive.

Longing
To belong.

Lost,
Found,
Lost again.
And I smile.

Beauty and perfection
Eyes, it was all in the eyes.

Magical night

Moonlit sky,
Silent whispers,
Enchanting,
Stars and moonbeams,
Twinkling dreams,
Fireflies and shadows,
Night's embrace.

Endless wonders,
Peaceful slumber.

Serenade.

MAGIC NIGHT.

Subtle yet bold.

Yearning,
To behold.

Lost,
Found,
Lost again,
Yet I sway.

Glow and grace,
Moon, it was all in the moon.

Embrace

Moonlight,
Gentle breeze,
Whispers,
Laughter and tears,
Whispers,
Dreams and fears,
Embracing both sides

Endless stories,
Silence speaks.

Serene.

EMBRACE.

Fragile yet resilient.

Seeking,
To be seen.

Lost,
Found,
Lost again,
Yet I dance.

Grace and flaws,
Soul, it was all in the soul.

Daydream

Love's warm glow,
Tender touch,
Endless hope,
Hearts and laughter,
Whispers of forever,
Butterflies and stardust,
Eternal dance.

Boundless joy,
Radiant beams.

Serenade.

Daydream.

Gentle and bright.

Yearning,
To take flight.

Lost,
Found,
Lost again,
Yet I soar.

Dreams take flight,
Light, it's all in the light.

Self-love

Loving oneself properly, a journey unique,
From diverse backgrounds, we all seek.
Here's how I love myself, from where I stand,
In this ever-changing, complex land.

I refuse mistreatment, I stand my ground,
No fights unworthy, no noise around.
I ponder long-term, is it worth the strife?
If not, I change within, to live a better life.

Clear communication, a bridge I build,
With those I cherish, conflicts I yield.
If respect lacks, I choose to depart,
No table worth sitting, if it breaks my heart.

I let go of hurt, I take no offense,
Others' behavior, not my defense.
I pause and breathe, when burdens weigh,
Restoring calmness, finding my way.

A home spa, a luxury I embrace,
Green spaces, where I find solace.
I work with purpose, not aimlessly,
Every effort counts, that's my decree.

Thoughtful responses, not impulsive deeds,
Balance and moderation, in all my needs.
Asking for help, without fear or shame,
Learning from rejection, not just the aim.

Surrounding myself, with love and growth,
Inspiring souls, in whom I betroth.
Caring for my body, its health I mind,
My temple sacred, my peace I find.

Exploring new paths, fueling my zeal,
Experiencing life, its highs and its feel.
Guiding others, as I learn anew,
In helping them, I find myself too.

Listening closely, to my inner voice,
Setting boundaries, it's my conscious choice.
Spending time alone, with myself I bond,

Filling my cup, before love's beyond.

So this is how I love, from deep within,
A journey ongoing, where I begin.
With each step forward, I embrace me tight,
In loving myself truly, I find my light

PART V
Reflection and Contemplation

Seekings

To forgive, I faced the mirror's gaze,
Seeing beyond the surface, into the depths of my ways.
I embraced my flaws, my demons and my angels,
Balancing them within, harmonizing their tangles.
Recognizing the pain I caused, big or small,
A humbling realization, embracing my fall.
Cowardice and mindlessness led me astray,
Following judgments, my own truth I'd betray.
Realizing my part, strength and wisdom were born,
Forgiving myself and others, their journeys to adorn.
For we are all human, flawed in our own way,
Each on a path, learning day by day.

9 789360 949150

Printed by Libri Plureos GmbH in Hamburg, Germany